Some Histories of the Sheffield Flood 1864

Rob Hindle

Templar Poetry

First Published 2006 by Templar Poetry

Templar Poetry
PO Box 7082
Bakewell
DE45 9AF

www.templarpoetry.co.uk

ISBN-13 978-0-9550023-4-2
ISBN-10 0-9550023-4-6

Copyright © Rob Hindle 2006

Rob Hindle has asserted his rights to be identified
as the author of this work in accordance
with the Copyright, Designs and Patents Act 1988.

All rights reserved. This book is sold subject to the condition
that it shall not, by way of trade or otherwise, be lent, resold, hired out
or otherwise circulated without the publisher's prior consent, in any form
of binding or cover other than that in which it is published and without
a similar condition including this condition being imposed on
the subsequent purchaser.

For permission to reprint or broadcast these poems write to
Templar Poetry

Typeset by Pliny
Graphics by Palloma Violet
Printed and bound in India

To the many people who died as a result of the bursting of the Dale Dyke Dam on 12 March, 1864.

ACKNOWLEDGEMENTS

Some of the poems published here have previously appeared in Staple and YAC YAC, to whom thanks are due.

All quotes are taken from Samuel Harrison, A Complete History of the Great Flood at Sheffield (1864).

Advertisements are taken from the Sheffield Telegraph and Sheffield Times (March 1864), reproduced on microfiche held in Sheffield City Libraries Local Studies Archive, Surrey Street, Sheffield.

FOREWORD

Shortly after midnight on 12th March 1864, the embankment of the newly-constructed Dale Dyke Dam north west of Sheffield burst, disgorging 600 million gallons of water into the Loxley and Don valleys in less than half an hour. Villages, farms and manufactories along the valleys, as well as the poor districts of Sheffield close to the Don, were inundated. Between 250 and 300 people were killed. In the days that followed, Samuel Harrison, the printer and reporter of the Sheffield Times, collected a vast amount of information about the victims and survivors of the Flood. At the same time, tens of thousands of day trippers travelled to Sheffield, eager to witness the devastation. It is due to the industry of the former and the morbid curiosity of the latter that so much material survives.

CONTENTS

Ann Trickett's Sampler	1
The Workhouse 1 - The Venereal Ward	3
Thomas Petty	5
Eliza Crownshaw	7
The Workhouse 2 - The Lunatic Wards	8
Tom Kay	10
Joseph and John Denton	11
Emma Wallace	13
Undertow	14
Alathea Hague	19
The Workhouse 3 - The Upper Room	22
Thomas Elston	23
Mrs	25
The Workhouse 4 - At the Boiler House	27
A Coal Monger	29
At Rotherham	31
Found Things	33
The Workhouse 5 - a Paper (damaged) found floating in the Governor's Office	35
CLOB	37
Epitaph to Henry Burkinshaw	39

Ann Trickett's Sampler (1815)

Found at Warren Vale, Rawmarsh, about 12 miles downstream from the Trickett farmhouse at Malin Bridge.

Bright red of poppies
for the grapes round the border.
Red too for the pots of roses.
She has never seen grapes
or heard the word terracotta.

The verses worry her.
The Lord my pasture shall prepare
disturbs her work. On the hill
the sharp, bare shapes of trees
shake at an empty sky.

And guard me with a watchful eye.
She bends close, working the bright gold
of birds below her name.
The words of the psalm are black
and rigid. *In the paths of death I tread*

With gloomy horrors overspread.
There is a grand, strong house
with a portico and three broad steps
down to an avenue of limes.
There is a fishpond in a dark ground

with ducks on it, beaks touching
almost. Some sheep and deer
stand near the water. A dog is sniffing
the air, the short day's end.
And streams shall murmur all around.

The Workhouse 1 - The Venereal Ward

In the washroom at the far end of the ward
there is a row of copper basins hanging
from hooks along a lime washed wall.
The light is good though the window is small.

Each morning before the doctor comes
we must go to the washroom one by one
and fill our basin from a covered tank
and set it down by a drain in the ground.

Below the line of basin hooks are other hooks
holding towels and bags of thick, dark cloth.
We take our towel and place it on the lime washed
floor. We take our bag and pull from it

a brass syringe and a stoppered jar.
In the jar is a salve as thick and dark as blood:
the matron said it's cinnabar, raw mercury
that makes it red. That was a shock -

I'd thought mercury silver as moonlight.
The woman next to me was quiet last night
the first time in a week. I think her close
to death she is so still. They say it is poison

and kills those it cannot cure. I fear death
but more the pain of dying: so each day
washing my hands in the red stained bowl
I pray for my safety, or for a sudden end.

Thomas Petty
Stove Grate Maker, Victoria Gardens, Neepsend.

He sits in a kitchen chair like a drunk
gazing through the open door
and scraping his pipe clean endlessly.

The rain has channelled its own ditches
and runs now over clay and splintered
sandstone. All the soil's life is gone.

Near his feet is some crumpled kale
and the last few leeks. There is nothing
more for him until the sky is clear.

Fragments of ash drop slowly and stick
to his trousers and boots. Somewhere
near, there is a sound of the sea,

of someone trying to sweep water away.
Each night the man claws for a memory
of spring sun and the smell of digging;

but the water knocks and cackles
and all he sees is an old woman, bent low
in the shallows and searching for something.

THE FLOOD. --- MISSING, from Owlerton, SAMUEL SENIOR, aged 76 Years, Height about 5ft.8in., is without whiskers; has a slight Scar on the Upper Lip; and both his Hands have been injured. - Apply to WILLIAM SENIOR, Old Wire Mill, Thurgoland.

Eliza Crownshaw

A servant, newly started in employment at the Stag Inn, Malin Bridge

Laying her things out the night before she left
she forgot it was raining.
In the next room she heard her father's voice
like the deep voice of the house.
From her mother, nothing.

The mirror had been her grandmother's:
real cherry wood, though the silver had spotted.
She turned it towards the candle: it made a yellow
moon dance on the empty wall.

Twisting her hair up into her nape
she steadied the mirror. She would
hold the hair tight with the tortoiseshell comb
(there on the blanket like an amber crow's wing)
and wear a scarf against the bitter cold.

The voice had stopped. Remembering the rain,
she picked up her things and stepped to the window.
Though there was no moon, she traced
with her childhood the hills and the spating river
and the steep-dropping lane.

The Workhouse 2 - The Lunatic Wards

In here it is never quiet all night:
we sedate the worst of them and listen

not for madness but for something singular
or strange in the general din.

Mary, who paces from window to window
in the day watching the rain run down

lies still in bed seeing the same drops
dribble in the dark of her mind

so if her hectic commentary were to stop
that would be something strange.

And Ruth, whose nights are full of small shocks
which sit her up and leave her rocking,

her face squashed between her hands,
would raise alarm only if she failed to stir.

It is quiet now. Even the rain we curse
each morning has become the night's sound:

it soothes the nerves of some and
(God forgive us) drowns the cries of others.

Tom Kay

Went to live at his son-in-law's farm at Malin Bridge on the day of the flood, having buried his wife on the previous Wednesday.

Because she was older and felt the bitterness
in every wind, you seemed strong, a big man.
When you stood at the field gate watching
the horses, you drove your stick deep
into the ground. A bad back made you noisy
but poor hearing and sight left the world bruised
not bruising. If your coat dragged a cup
to the kitchen floor, you were already cursing
the ice in the yard or the rain-swollen door.

Dropping earth on her coffin your back seized up.
You refused your son's arm but agreed that
their lad would come round with a cart and fetch
your things over. They insisted you were settled
in your kitchen chair, but left soon after.
You sat and dozed and the fire burned down.
Something in your mind (not the sound of rain
or the clattering wind) shocked you out of sleep.
As you moved, pain moved. You felt tired, cold.

Joseph Denton (14)
John Denton (11)
Working the night shift at Loxley Old Forge

Last spring we went nesting in Agden Wood.
I stood in the leaf-mush - my back not fit
after three winters' work - and watched you
climb. The rooks sprayed like shot and I heard
you laughing. When you dropped back beside me,
mouthed a piebald egg into my palm, your hair
was hung with lime white shit. Lucky.

In the autumn you came to the forge with me.
The lads broke you in with their filthy tales
but the way they spat blood was the bigger shock.
You liked the night shift - the dawn's walk home,
the flaring shadows (though the tilt hammer's thump
couldn't stifle the hack of the grinders' cough).

You climbed the high birches and still
had the breath to suck out the yolk.
Now the work of the winter was making you curse.
When the dam wall burst and the night caved in,
you shot up the shuttle pole while I stood there
gaping. I thought of the rook's egg clutched in
your grin. Then nothing.

INTERNMENT OF THE DEAD.
I hereby give Public Notice, that the REMAINS OF ALL THE PERSONS found DROWNED will be interred THIS DAY (Monday, the 14th March), unless, in the meantime, they are
identified and removed by their Friends.

THOMAS JESSOP, Mayor.
Sheffield, 12th. March 1864.

Emma Wallace

'Poor old widow' and mother of two, Cotton Mill Row, Kelham.

Not old, though she looked fifty
with her hair white and the hollows of her eyes.
She shook with the palsy, so that when
she stood at her door at each shift-end
it looked like she was counting us home.

George had worked on the Manchester railway.
When they ran the first train up the valley
to Woodhead, he wiped the smuts into his eyes
with his fists. He left the night their daughter was born,
smashing the yard door like it was someone's face.

Emma stayed indoors for a month. Later
she said she was better off without him.
At night you could hear her talking to herself
or dragging a chair across to the window.
Her children were silent and not much seen.

The night of the flood she didn't last long.
The lad upstairs made a rope from a sheet
but the stinking river soon carried her off.
We pulled out the children and made them a bed up:
sleeping, they both look the spit of their father.

Undertow

'Stranger still was the case of a man who, earlier that day, had attempted to commit suicide by throwing himself into the river. He was fished out and locked in a cell at Hillsborough police station, pending an appearance in court. When the flood rushed into the building and began to rise alarmingly he no longer relished the idea of sudden departure by immersion and shouted to be let out. Inspector Thomas Smalley and his wife, Victoria, sleeping in a room above the lock up, were aroused by the commotion and, by the time the policeman got to the screaming prisoner, the water was up to his armpits. With difficulty, Smalley rescued the man who by now was trembling and appeared to have abandoned all thoughts of a self inflicted demise. The inspector, who spent the remainder of that night and the following few days assisting the many sufferers in the area, caught a chill. He confided to his wife and his doctor: 'I got my death on the night of the flood and shall never get better.' His premonition was sadly accurate. He also contracted typhus (probably through swallowing dirty water) and died two months after saving a man who, for a time at least, had not wanted to live.'

I Thanatos

She drinks too much.
Her breath reeks
of it and she has that blotchy look.
She never blinks.

She has the nose for it,
can sniff it a mile off.

It gets her livid:
enough is never enough.

Here's one coming.
Not ripe, quite
but still that tang of hopelessness.
Come on luvvy, that's right.

He jumps quickly from the parapet
and is engulfed, pulled down
by the heavy rush of the undertow.

An early windfall.
Get 'em sharp before the bloom
brings birds, flies, worms.
He surfaces fifty feet downstream.

She's better swimming.
The water bears her flooded
body, makes her young again.
She feels the blood

in her face, her heart
squeezed under her thick skin.

Through watery eyes
she spots him

rucked against the weir lip.
He's face up, sucking at the air.

*Two men, walking the banks,
discover him and, at great peril
to themselves, traverse the weir.*

She licks wet lips.
The bitter taste is still there.

II Eros

Winter is a good time.
No rush, just the steady drop
of the sick and the old.
Then a night like this comes up.

Five years' worth of rain
in half an hour and the town
asleep. Pigs, cattle, sheep,
families and those living alone;

a drunken pair stopped on a bridge,
mouths dropped and hands in fists;
a man with money and a woman
out for one more job. She's missed

later, but only by her gentlemen.
Now, who's this? That's right,
my dear, we've met.

The man, locked in his cell, cries out
for assistance. Nothing.

The inundation stinks around him.
There, then, love, be calm -
you were looking for me, remember?

The inspector unlocks the door into the dark.
Holding a lantern by his head
he descends the stairs into the churning cold.

The man is flat against the wall,
arms spread as if in chains
or nailed to a beam. *The smell*
is worse than the water
and stings in the officer's eyes.
He drags the man from the flooded room.

She is in the doorway watching
the men choke ooze and filth onto the path.
The weaker is oblivious to his luck
and curses as he spits.

The other sees a thing in the shadows
and clamps his teeth, feeling the river grit
between them. The flood noise fades
and he is gone far out into the night.

Alathea Hague

A domestic servant (17?) employed by the Chapman family at Little Matlock

No roar
no whistle or scream
just smack like a hammer
a black hole
where the house had been

Lazy you spin
a stunned Pre-Raphaelite
drugged gaze
and hair spread thick
on the skin of the river

Quiet again
you are better now
than those downstream
awake and something coming
in the dark

The sky lightens slowly
Those searching the sludge
see the trails your feet make
against the current

They string out on a rope

and inch towards you
The front man
sunk to his belly in cold
grasps your wrist

shouts

thrashes backwards
and he and you are hauled up
to the empty world

You lie in the lane
they stoop on walls
and shoulders
getting their breath

FOUND, at Hillfoot, a Little STORE PIG.
The owner may have the same by applying to Isaac Clark, Wellington Inn, Langsett road.

The Workhouse 3 - The Upper Room

'A large proportion of the dead were conveyed to the Sheffield Workhouse, and there laid out for identification.'

Only two candles light the upper room.
One is on a ledge by the door, for use
of the constable when the families come.

He sits in a chair trying not to lose
his mind. Back turned to the emptiness
he watches desperately the flaring shadows

pattering the wall. All night the dead lie
waiting, some craning stiffly towards the door.
Others, hopeless, turn the other way.

There, the second candle burns with a perfect flame.
In its light a man writes slowly, the scratch of his pen
calling each still shape its first and last name.

Thomas Elston

Grinder, Neepsend Nursery Gardens. One of four examined in the Inquest into the flood.

They have put me on a stone table
and covered me. Three others lie
nearby. I think it is the mortuary.

It is as dark as a well, but with no
echo, and there is not the smallest
light, nor breeze, nor chill.

Death is simple, it seems. I am
here and there is nothing of life
left in me except the memory of it

which, though bright and sharp
as a coin, remains to me only as
the diary of an ancient ancestor.

I remember seeing death in others
and thought it difficult then - a clot
coughed into the hand, maybe,

or a shared glance seen by one
dragged broken from a machine.
But that was dying, not death

and though smashed down
by a stupid and terrific force
and, dying, glimpsed through the

broken door my wife, face up
and floating round and round,
I am dead now and there's an end.

Mrs

MISSING, and supposed to be Drowned in the Flood, a MARRIED WOMAN, Light Complexion, Slender Form, one Little Finger deformed, height about 5 feet 2½ Inches, Age 33. Her Relatives earnestly request that, on her discovery, Information thereof be given to Mr. Waterhouse, Whittington moor, Chesterfield.

You said it curled like barley twist
which was so much nonsense I took it in.
My grandmother wept at the wedding
and drank too much. 'You know she's cursed,'
she said to anyone. Your smile
when it reached me was a little thin.

Things happened. Two sons, two daughters
(both tall like you and with perfect hands).
We became respectable. When grandmother
died you read the psalm at her graveside.
I looked up while everyone was bowed in prayer
but the afternoon sun put your face in shade.

The gloves I wore that day I'd spent
the morning on, unpicking and then re-stitching
with fine black thread, so my finger
with its rutted skin could feel the smooth gold
you wrapped its neighbour in. Another thing
my grandmother swore by: gold is for healing.

I took your name with my vows. It is just
yours now: I am again deformed, original.
The ring is polished by the silt I am quilted in
while the river prepares me for burial,
its strong, expert hands softening my limbs,
smoothing the skin of all my fingers.

The Workhouse 4 - At the Boiler House

'The inmates were all in bed, except a young man in charge of the boiler house. He is an imbecile, and is known by the name of "George." The water came rushing in with such fury that "George" got on the top of the boiler house in order to ensure his own personal safety. That accomplished, he does not seem to have had the sense to take measures for the protection of others. There he sat on the boiler house, whistling.'

On that night I saw ghosts,
scores of them, sailing
below me in the dark
and though they did not look
at me, I heard them talking
as they drifted by.

There was a little child
on her mother's belly
and she was asking why
they had woken her from sleep
and where did they go
and no-one knew.

An old man held
the soft ghost of his dog,
mumbling comforts
and stroking the wet fur.
The dog wagged its tail,
nuzzled into the old man's hair.

A whole family
the father still clinging
to the frame of a bed
and calling back to his wife
at the end of a long string
of children, fearing her dead.

On cold days in the yard
Mister Wescoe would say
Whistle, George and keep
your spirits up. And I sat
all that long night and whistled,
whistled on the boiler house top.

A Coal Monger

A six-yard hole made your place a picture.
I think I expected a dragon's nest,
the locked box you slept on sunk thigh-deep
in coal heaped high as a rich man's ransom.

In this light and mud there is nothing to show
but a lantern hung from a hook in the roof
and the top five feet of an empty wall.
I think it was clean, though, your life.

You were one of those dumped at the Wicker arch
(even then, your nails were clean as peel).
Your box was found in a neighbour's yard
(he craned to look as the lock was sprung):

just some blankets and a tin with letters in it.

BOROUGH OF SHEFFIELD. LIME AND CHLORIDE OF LIME To be had, Free of Charge on application at the HIGHWAY OFFICE YARD, Bower spring; and at the HIGHWAY OFFICE, Nursery street, Wicker.

By order of the Health Committee.

R. CHAPMAN, Chief Sanitary Inspector.

Council Hall, 18th March, 1864.

At Rotherham

Mary Appleby's night-dress
is snagged on a rock below Rotherham Bridge

and has caught the attention of Police Sergeant Ireland
who's been up all night and is crossing the bridge

to the Masbro side. Four hours ago
he was running up Bridgegate in the black and rain

and the river (he thought) set to flood the town out.
As he stops the stink catches in his throat.

For the past four hours
the river's been rocking Mary Appleby's

body out of her night-dress. From Rotherham Bridge
Sergeant Ireland can't see this and turns

on his way, his still wet notebook
holding the night's dead close to his chest.

Mary Appleby's body is later recovered
from a flooded garden and wheeled

to the station on a creaking cart.
Police Sergeant Ireland has finished his shift

and has fallen asleep at the kitchen table -
with his tea in his hand, his wife later said

(though she kept to herself how she gently
undressed him and got him to bed.)

Found Things

a file cutter's stool
two legs broken
two missing

a brass dog collar
an inscription on its rim

two porcelain figures
(Charles II and Queen)

they stare down at
something

a doll's basket

a gold chain with a locket

a razor
the blade held tight in its handle

a bible
bulging like a rich man's purse

a cigar case
no cigar

a child's battledore
(we'd call it a racket)
carved like a heart
or the ace of spades

a rocking chair

a nicely framed picture
the SS Great Eastern
in full steam and sail
(on a wall in Bridge Street)

a stick
the handle pale with wear

a snuff box full
of its dark sour smell

The Workhouse 5 - A Paper (damaged) found floating in the Governor's Office

Any pauper who shall neglect

    who shall make any noise when silence is ordered to be kept
                use obscene   or profane language
                by word or deed insult or revile

        not duly cleanse his person

        pretend sickness
        play at   games of chance

SHALL BE DEEMED DISORDERLY

Any pauper who shall wilfully disobey any lawful order
        mischievously damage or soil any property

        shall be drunk
           commit any act of indecency
Or   wilfully disturb the other inmates

SHALL BE DEEMED REFRACTORY

No distinguishing mark of disgrace to be worn by any adult pauper unless such pauper shall be called disorderly or refractory

THE GREAT FLOOD AT LOXLEY. JOSHUA WOODWARD, OLIVE PAPER-MILLS, begs to inform the Merchants and Manufacturers of Sheffield that the Stock Rooms containing his Stock of OLD ROPE PAPER is not in the least damaged.

CLOB

(Centre Line of Old Bank - inscribed on memorial stones to indicate the site of the original Dale Dyke embankment)

'A large number of persons went as far as the reservoir to see the gap in the embankment. The photographers were busy at all the most picturesque parts, and have produced faithful representations of many objects of interest.'

March, 2005

On the bridge there's snow, a dog's prints.
I'm here, muddy with searching for four white stones.
The river is comfortingly clear and moving softly
but there's an urgent hissing somewhere.

Up steps on the other side the noise grows.
There is a white flatness through the trees
like an empty field on end. Then the racket:
a cast iron pipe thunders water at the gorge.

At the top of the wood, a long straight line
on a wall of snow. The reservoir beyond;
a wagtail dipping in the slush of the outflow.
There is nothing here, just the edge of it all.

I could cut across the bank top, scare myself
with the steep slope down; but the day shows
snow pools deeper than my shoes. I pick
my way back into the valley's shadow

and up through the pines. Near the road
the plaque I saw when I arrived; close by, a stone,
one of those I was searching for but missed
not thinking the old bank would have been this high.

Epitaph for Henry Burkinshaw

Here lies Harry
a Sheffield navvy
hard grafter
solid drinker.

He lodged at Damflask
near the river
drank in the Barrel
and retired early.

Downing his last one
someone said
The dam wall's cracked:
a lad's gone down
for the engineer.
Harry laughed
and left for his bed.

Here lies Harry
Sheffield navvy
drowned in bed
his body found
below the weir
one stocking on.